Dream It, Dare It, Do It

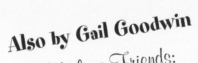

Also by Gail Goodwin

Fabulous Friends:
A Celebration of Girlfriendship

Dream It, Dare It, Do It

Reach for the Stars, Girlfriends!

Gail Goodwin

Text by P. L. Stein

**Andrews McMeel
Publishing**

Kansas City

Dream It, Dare It, Do It

06 07 08 09 10 WKT 10 9 8 7 6 5 4 3 2 1

ISBN-13: 978-0-7407-5827-0
ISBN-10: 0-7407-5827-6

Library of Congress Control Number: 2005933864

www.andrewsmcmeel.com

ATTENTION: SCHOOLS AND BUSINESSES

Dream It,
Dare It, Do It

Having a **dream** is a **fabulous** thing.

When you dare to
make a dream come alive,
you feel like **shouting out,**

"Hey world, look at me!"

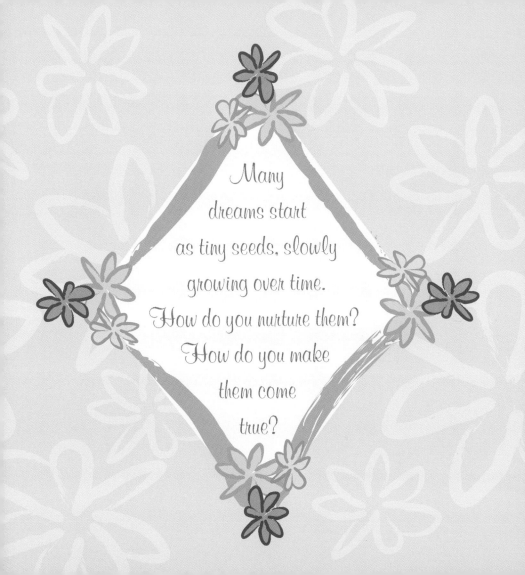

Many
dreams start
as tiny seeds, slowly
growing over time.
How do you nurture them?
How do you make
them come
true?

So glad you asked!

First, it's wise to take a good,
long look at yourself.

It's obvious you're a special person, someone who feels things deeply

and cares about others.

Plus, you've got that certain drive.

It helps, too, that you can laugh about how amazing, absurd, and wonderful life is.

Once you know yourself well,
it's time to truly define your one and only,
utterly unique,

Beautiful
Dream.

Creating a goal can be satisfying and fun,
but you also need a few other things,
like inspiration.

preparation,

and
perspiration!

Throw in a positive attitude and you're ready

Star

to go
for it!

(A new outfit
may not help a whole lot,
but it can't hurt.)

Committing to a goal is a big deal,
so it's perfectly normal to feel a bit timid

or a **little** scared.

But never forget:
Whatever your dream is,
you have the power to make it come true.
That power has always,
always been inside you.

Believe it, honey!

Goals are funny things.
Sometimes they seem so far off,
it feels like no map can show you the way.

Other times, you may feel an
idea growing inside, but you're not
sure what it will become.

A little "me" time can help
sort things out.

The main thing
is to keep your eyes
on the prize.

Roll toward the goal.

Lean to the dream.

In other words—

stay focused, sweetie.

When you
put your heart into
something, it's natural to
feel there's a lot
on the line.

So let's **think** about **that.**
Who are you, really?

*Well, for starters,
you're kind.*

It's fun to do everything with you . . . or nothing at all.

You're the best
kind of silly,

XOXO...

a real sweetie.

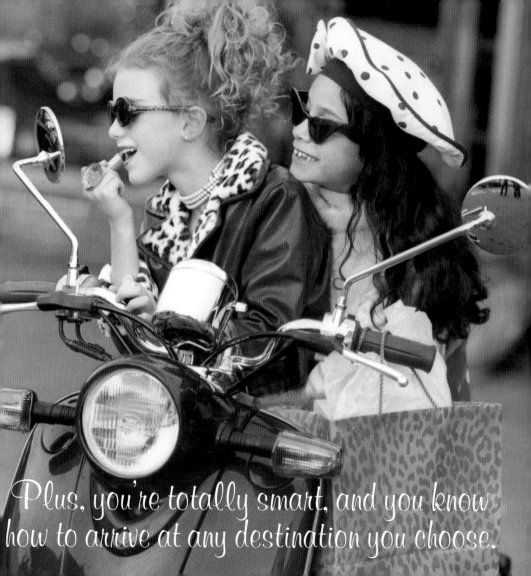

Plus, you're totally smart, and you know how to arrive at any destination you choose.

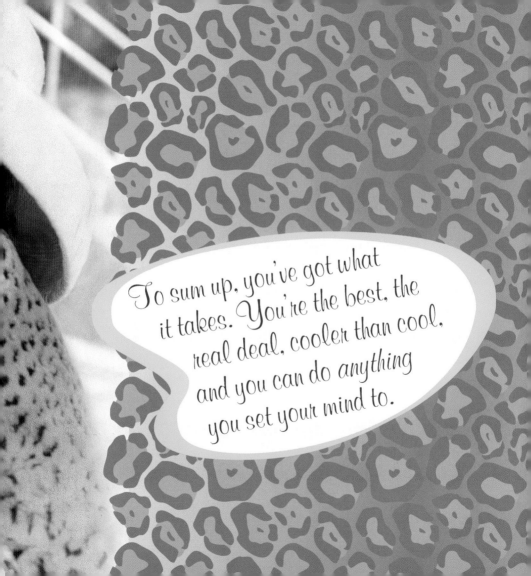

Magical things will begin to happen.

But please don't worry if you lose momentum or get off track.

We all have our ups

and our downs.

If at first you
don't succeed,

take a soak in a
nice hot tub,

nourish
yourself,

and try,
try again!

If you start to feel
like the sky's the limit

and you can fly higher than
you ever imagined–

good call!

Just a quick word on the naysayers—
those people who may not believe
in your dream as much as you do.

Simply tell them, gently but firmly, to go fly a kite.

It's far better to surround yourself with a supportive circle of friends.

Aim as high as your wonderful heart takes you.

Because this
is your life.
It's not a dress rehearsal,

You're all *set!*

If you
dream it,

if **you** dare it,

you can do it!